From Workshop to Warfare
The lives of medieval women

Carol Adams, Paula Bartley,
Hilary Bourdillon, Cathy Loxton

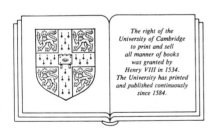

The right of the
University of Cambridge
to print and sell
all manner of books
was granted by
Henry VIII in 1534.
The University has printed
and published continuously
since 1584.

Cambridge University Press

Cambridge
New York   Port Chester
Melbourne   Sydney

A note on money in this book

£1 = 20s (shillings)
1s = 12d (pence)
1 mark = about 13s 4d

The currency in the later medieval period was pounds, shillings and pence, but marks were also used. The old shilling has become 5 new pence. Remember that the value of money was very different at this time. To work out the real value you should compare the wages people received with how much they had to pay for rent, food, clothes, etc.

The authors would like to thank Nicole Stone for her initial picture research and support.

Front cover A lady defending herself and her household from attack. From a French manuscript, late 15th century.

Published by the Press Syndicate of the University of Cambridge
The Pitt Building, Trumpington Street, Cambridge CB2 1RP
40 West 20th Street, New York, NY 10011, USA
10 Stamford Road, Oakleigh, Melbourne 3166, Australia

© Cambridge University Press 1990

First published 1983
New edition published 1990

Printed in Great Britain by the University Press, Cambridge

British Library cataloguing in publication data
From Workshop to Warfare: the lives of medieval women/Carol Adams
Women in history.
1. England. Society. Role of women, 1200–1500. For schools
I. Adams, Carol, 1948–   II. Series
305.420942

ISBN 0-521-39983-1

Library of Congress cataloging-in-publication data
From Workshop to Warfare: the lives of medieval women/Carol Adams
... [et al]. – New ed.
   p. cm.
   Includes bibliographical references
   Contents: Finding out about medieval women – Living in the Middle Ages – The lady of the manor – The nun in the convent – Women at work – Women law-breakers.
   ISBN 0-521-39983-1
   1. Women – History – Middle Ages. 500–1500. I. Adams, Carol.
HQ1143.F76   1990
305.4′09′02—dc20   90-36078
                                                     CIP

UP

Contents

What impression do these pictures give you of women's lives in the Middle Ages? These are typical examples of the view of medieval women found in many books. From the Book of Hours *produced in Rouen in the 1480s.*

iv

1 Finding out about medieval women

How many books have you ever read that look at the part women have played in the past? The next time you are in the library or looking at history books check to see how often women are mentioned in the text, the chapter headings, the title, the pictures. How many books about the Middle Ages give you the impression that the peasant woman was only concerned with the home? How many give you the idea that the upper-class lady worked at her tapestry, and spent her time gazing from the castle turret at handsome princes?

This book shows what an important role women played in the Middle Ages.

Searching for information

There is a great deal of work to be done before we have a complete picture of the part women played during this period of history. Here are some of the common problems which arose when this book was written.

Many historians have been men and have tended to ignore women's lives.

Most documents describe the activities of a very small number of people who governed the country, or owned land.

Much of the literature of the later Middle Ages, written for the aristocracy, gives a romantic view of the lady; fair in looks and manners, she commands the love and devotion of her Knight. This idealised picture of women is also found in the illustrations in medieval manuscripts.

The lives of ordinary people are difficult to uncover. Few peasants could read or write, so they have left no diaries or descriptions of their lives. We do have some accounts written by upper-class ladies, but these are few.

When you look at pictures of medieval life it is often hard to tell whether people are men or women since both often wore long flowing gowns.

Most of the original evidence is written in Latin or French. The script (handwriting) may at first be difficult to read.

Many primary sources have been lost or destroyed. For example many of the guild records were burnt in the Great Fire of London in 1666.

Both books and pictures are often held in libraries which are not easy to get into. You may need special permission to use them and they may only be open during the working day.

Sometimes the document you need to look at is not available because it is being repaired.

The Middle Ages lasted for several hundred years. Most of the material in this book covers the years 1300–1500. What may be true of women in the later Middle Ages is not necessarily true of women in earlier years.

The sources

In spite of these difficulties, it is possible to find out about how women lived in the Middle Ages. Upper-class women wrote letters and made wills which contain lots of vivid information about their lives. There are also household account books and other evidence from domestic as well as business records. By looking closely at the records of manor courts and local law courts, it is possible to see women playing an active part in legal disputes and offences against the law. Other important and useful sources include reports made by Bishops visiting nunneries. Among the visual evidence of everyday life, women can be found doing all sorts of jobs usually considered to have been 'men's work'. A few modern historians have written books about the Middle Ages which include information about women. These are also very useful sources.

This book presents just some of the evidence which we found to be interesting and often very unexpected, but it is by no means the end of the story.

2 Living in the Middle Ages

How the land was divided up

The king owned all the land, but gave some of it to his barons in return for loyalty and military service. If you look at the diagram you will see how the barons, and knights in turn, shared out their lands. This system is known as the feudal system.

Medieval kings had to protect their people and their land. Many wanted to increase the amount of land they ruled. This meant that war was a way of life for the men of the nobility. Wars were fought against other states, local wars were fought against rivals and religious wars against non Christians. A strong and loyal army was necessary to help the king rule his country.

The Christian Church

After the king, the Church was the biggest landholder. This meant that the Church was an important and powerful force. Most people in Western Europe had the same religious beliefs, and people were strongly influenced by the teachings of the Church and the stories they were told from the Bible.

The Church taught that women should obey their husbands.

Wives, submit yourselves unto your own husbands, as unto the Lord. For the husband is head of the wife, even as Christ is head of the Church   *St Paul*

The Church had two very different ideas about women. Priests would tell their

OWNERSHIP OF LAND

whole country   king

great lords   bishops

great/large estates

small/local estates

lesser lords   clergy

strips of land   peasants

This is how medieval society is usually shown in school-books. Who is missing from this picture?

An illustration, from a 15th century French manuscript of avarice (greed), one of the seven deadly sins. In medieval manuscripts, sin is more often shown as female than as male. Can you think of any reason for this? What are the six other deadly sins?

congregations that Eve, a woman, had brought sin into the world. Towards the end of the Middle Ages, in 1487, the *Malleus Maleficarum*, a book which tried to explain the origins of evil, claimed that women were deceitful and told lies.

There is a defect in the formation of woman since she was formed from a bent rib...through this defect she is an imperfect animal, she always deceives.

But the Church also taught that women should be pure and holy like the Virgin Mary, the mother of Christ. According to the teachings of the Church, women should lead sheltered and protected lives and should be kept away from the affairs of the wicked world.

Marriage

Another control on women's lives was marriage. Since wealth was based on owning land and was passed down through families, people did not usually marry for love. Marriages were arranged by parents to increase the family's land, power, wealth and influence. The peasant woman as well as the lady would have her marriage arranged for her; and then the lord of the manor had an interest, because he received a fee whenever someone on his land got married.

People had to make sure they could support a family before they married. Before marriage, a woman was looked after by her parents or guardian. When she married she accepted her husband as her master.

A widow, on the other hand, was in a much stronger position than married women, since she automatically received her 'widows dower'. This was one-third of her husband's lands. She also had her dowry returned on her husband's death. This was the money or property her family paid her husband when she married. However, she was likely to come under strong pressure to remarry. Men wanted to marry her for her money, and her feudal lord feared that she could not look after her lands alone.

Having children

Once married, women of all ranks, rich or poor, spent most of their lives bearing or raising children. Blanche of Castile, who married Prince Louis (the future Louis VIII of France) in 1200, gave birth twelve times. Royal children received the best care available; but even so, seven out of her twelve babies died at birth, and only three lived to maturity.

Today, the average number of children in a family in Britain is 1.8. We do not know the size of the family in medieval Britain. No chroniclers have listed the names of the peasants' children to tell us how many survived and how many died. We do know that the death rate was very high among children. Young people, living in, say, 1342 would already have attended the funeral of several brothers and sisters. Women were frequently pregnant, in some cases giving birth seventeen times or more, but families were not necessarily large.

L'lan de nreseigne
mul œnt quatre higz
et sept ou mois
daoust acoucha la royne de frā
ce elysabeth la fille du conte de
henau dun filz en la cite de
paris lequel fut nomme en
son nom de baptesme louys
Duquel la uertueuse iuuene

4   *Attending a birth. From a French manuscript, 15th century.*

A woman nurses her baby and cooks the food with the help of her child. From a Flemish manuscript, early 14th century.

In an age when there was no effective contraception, pregnancy was almost impossible to avoid. Rich or poor, women suffered and were injured in child birth; often they died. Despite this suffering, children were vitally important. In peasant families the more children there were, the more helpers there would be to bring in an income. Boys were more highly valued than girls, since people were very concerned about producing a son who would inherit their land.

In the following entry, taken from Church court records, the case came before the court because the child had been twice baptised. This was considered a sin. The entry also gives us a glimpse into the private fears medieval women had and the lengths they went to in order to provide their husbands with a son.

It was confirmed by Richard and Ida that when Ella pretended to be pregnant by Richard Beynghan her husband, they bought in the house of Adam Cockel of Bannebury for the price of twelve pence [12d] and a loaf of bread and a dish of bacon a male child who was supposed to have been born from the womb of Ella, and they had this child baptised at Scheynden, not knowing that he had already been baptised at Bannebury *Worcester, 1298*

All the people involved in the case were banished from the Church (excommunicated).

After a woman gave birth she had to be purified (blessed by the priest) before she could leave her house. A woman found not to have been purified was fined.

Joan Talbot has a child before marriage and leaves the place where she gave birth before being purified. She appeared on 16 November and is ordered to precede [go in front of] the procession in the parish of St. Denis on three Sundays, with her feet bare, in a gown, with a knotted handkerchief covering her head *London, 1475*

But whilst marriage and having children was an important part of women's lives, both rich and poor women played many other essential roles in society.

3   The lady of the manor

Women taking their husbands' place

Most women from the upper classes led very busy, active, and sometimes dangerous lives, running manors, farms and castles single-handed. This was because wealthy men spent most of their time away from home – travelling to and from their many estates, attending the king's court and fighting against neighbouring lords or in wars abroad. While they were away their wives took charge and ran the estates. Often they lived in isolated places and had no-one to rely on but themselves. There was no strong central government as today, and landowning families had great power over the local people. The lady of the manor was an influential person who had to deal with the management of acres of land, crops, animals, and property; hundreds of employees and their homes; legal arguments, fights, riots and even armed attacks. She certainly had to be strong and very capable.

A French woman, Christine de Pisan, writing in the later Middle Ages tells us a good deal about women's lives. Having been widowed at the age of twenty five with three young children, she earned her living as a writer. Unlike most writers at that time, she believed in women's rights and worked hard to encourage a positive view of women:

They say no evil is equal to a woman. But women slay [kill] no men, destroy no cities, do not oppress folk, betray realms, poison and set fire, or make false contracts. They are loving, gentle, charitable, modest, discreet.

She also described the many valuable things women did throughout society. In one book she said:

Because that knights, squires and gentlemen go upon journeys and follow the wars, it beseemeth [is necessary for] wives to be wise in all they do, for that most often they dwell [live] at home without their husbands who are at court or in divers [many different] lands.   *Christine de Pisan*

Margaret Paston

Margaret Paston was a lady of the manor who led a very interesting life, and we know a great deal about her from the letters she wrote. She lived in England in the fifteenth century, and her letters were written between 1441 and 1447.

She was a rich heiress who inherited all her father's estates in Norfolk. She was married to Sir John Paston, a lawyer, who spent several months each year away in London at the law courts. Several times he went to prison over legal arguments and she had to arrange for his release. During his absence, Margaret was left in charge of the huge estates, including several castles and manor houses, farmlands, forests, and the many tenants who lived on the estates.

A French woman, Christine of Pisan, earning her living as a writer. From the Collected Works of Christine de Pisan, *French, 15th century.*

6

This picture is from a French manuscript, late 15th century. It shows some of the many people who lived and worked on an estate. They were all supervised by the lady of the manor when her husband was away. Many pictures that show life in the Middle Ages are taken from religious stories. This is one of them. How can this picture help us to understand about life in the Middle Ages?

Her job was responsible, difficult and sometimes dangerous, because there were others who wanted Sir John's lands and these enemies had their own private armies. There are 104 letters surviving which Margaret wrote to her husband and they tell us about her busy life.

Running the estates: everyday problems

One of Margaret's problems was keeping the tenant's houses in repair because they were too poor to do it for themselves. This letter tells us how she managed to solve the problem:

There be divers [many] of your tenantries [tenancies] at Mautby that had great need to be repaired, and the tenants be so poor that they are not a power [able] to repair them; wherefore I would that the marsh might be kept in your own hand [by you] this year that the tenants might have rushes to repair with their houses. And also there is windfall wood at the manor that is of no great value that might help them with toward the reparation [repairs].

She had to sort out complaints and legal disagreements at the local law courts. In this letter she asked her husband to talk to the judges before they came to hold the court, because she knew there would be problems:

I suppose there shall be great labour [argument] against you and your servants at the assizes [law courts] and sessions here... it were well that ye should speak with the justices ere [before] they come here; and if ye will [wish] that I complain to them I will do as you advise me to do.

She had to buy and sell animals and obviously knew what she was doing.

There be bought for you three horses at St Faith's Fair, and all be trotters – right fair horses, and they be well kept.

7

She had to supervise renting out the lands and property to tenants, rather like a modern estate agent:

Your mills at Hellesdon be let for 12 marks and Richard Calle [the head bailiff] has let all your lands at Caister; but as for Mautby lands, they be not let yet.

Not everything went smoothly. She sometimes had problems with bad workers:

I pray you that ye will essay [try] to get some man at Caister to keep [look after] your buttery [food store] for the man that ye left with me will not take upon him to [do] daily as ye commanded.

Under attack

Margaret Paston organised the defence of the estates when they were attacked by armed soldiers. On one occasion, Sir John went to London leaving Margaret in charge of a garrison of soldiers inside the manor. It was attacked and invaded by soldiers who then carried Margaret outside and looted the place.

As far as we know she was not hurt, but it must have been very frightening. At one time she wrote to John asking him to supply bows and arrows to defend herself and her household.

A lady might have to defend herself and her household against attack. From a French manuscript, late 15th century.

Women (on the right) are defending their castle with bow and crossbow; men (on the left) are attacking. The two pictures are from an English manuscript, 14th century.

I pray you to get some crossbows and windlases [winders] to bend them with and quarrel [arrows]. And also I would ye should get two or three short poleaxes [battleaxes] to keep with doors [indoors] and as many jacks [jacket-armours] as ye may.

Margaret described the attacks that were often made on Sir John's houses. She took over as leader of the men when this happened, and called herself the 'captainess' of the castle. She was often in danger but had to act bravely and could not run away, as this description shows:

Great affrays [attacks] have been made upon me and my fellowship here on Monday last past. The Duke of Suffolk's men, with a 60 persons or more by estimation, and the tenants of the same town, some of them having rusty poleaxes and bills [spears] came into the manor yard...

Margaret saw much of her family's wealth and property destroyed and she had to face the job of repairing the damages and buying new things:

The Duke's men ransacked the church and bare away all the goods that was left there, both of ours and the tenants...The lodge and the remnant [rest] of your place was beaten down on Tuesday and Wednesday. I shall send you the bills.

It is quite clear from these letters that it was no easy life resisting attacks and facing armed seige without her husband there to share the burden:

It is too horrible a cost and trouble that we have now daily, and must have til it be otherwise; and your men dare not go about to gather up your livelihood [farm the land], and we keep here daily more than three hundred persons for savation [safety].

What happened to Margaret Paston was by no means exceptional and there are other examples of women defending their castles under seige. Joan Pelham wrote to her husband in 1399 from Pevensey Castle. He was in charge of the castle, but was away when his enemies attacked it:

And my dear lord, if it like you for to know of my fare [how I am], I am here belayed in manner of seige, with the county of Sussex, Surrey and a great parcel of Kent, so that I ne may not out, nor none victuals [food] get me, but with much hardship.

Running the household

A medieval lady was responsible for running a household of hundreds of people – servants, relatives, visitors, friends and family. She had to feed, entertain and put them up. She also had to supervise the preparation of huge amounts of food and other household goods. Beer, honey for sweetening, medicines, bread, cheese, butter and cloth were all made from raw materials produced on the estates. The lady's job must have been something like managing a large hotel today. These extracts show how a lady of the manor ran a large household at Acton in Suffolk in 1412 or 1413. Because it was the harvest season there were extra people to feed; the tenants on the estates had to be given their meals in return for their work bringing in the harvest.

WEDNESDAY, 9 AUGUST

(Guests) The bailiff of the manor with the harvest reeve and 14 of the household of the manor, John Scoyl with 30 boon-workers, John Holbrook, John Saltwell with his wife, one repast [meal].

Hunting was a popular pastime for upper-class women. The lady in this party is hawking. From an English manuscript, early 14th century.

PANTRY 40 white, and 4 black, loaves, and 14 loaves for the boon-workers; wine from supply; ale from stock.

KITCHEN 60 white herrings and 1½ salt fish.

PURCHASES 15 plaice and 16 soles 10½d., milk and cream 3d.

PROVENDER hay from stock for 6 horses; fodder for the same, one bush. of oats. Sum of purchases, 13½d.

MEALS: Breakfast 4, dinner 40, supper 3.

THURSDAY 10 AUGUST

(Guests) Sir Andrew Boteler with his wife, maidservant, chaplain, squire and 2 grooms, Agnes Whyte, 2 women of Sudbury, 2 men of Sudbury, 8 boon-workers, one repast, Saltwell with his wife, 8 boon-workers, the whole day.

PANTRY 56 white, and 8 black, loaves, and 10 loaves for the boon-workers; wine from supply; ale from stock.

KITCHEN one quarter of bacon, 26 pigeons, one joint of mutton, one heron.

PURCHASES eggs 8d.

PROVENDER hay from stock for 5 horses; fodder for the same, 3 pk. oats. Sum of purchases, 8d.

MEALS: Breakfast 8, dinner 30 Supper 30.

> *The Household Book of Dame Alice de Bryene*

A lady had to keep an eye on her servants to make sure they worked hard. From a Flemish manuscript, 1475.

Not all food could be produced on the estate and some things had to be bought, either from local market towns or ordered from London. Margaret Paston often asked her husband to buy things in London:

I pray you that ye will buy for me 1 lb of almonds and 1 lb of sugar, some freize [material] to maken of your childer's [children's] gowns. Ye shall have best cheap and best choice of Hay's wife, as it is told me. And that ye would buy a yarn of broadcloth of black for an hood for me, of 44d or 4s a yard   *Paston Letters*

Part of a housewife's job in those days was to get ready stores of food to be salted for the winter months when there was no fresh food. In this note Margaret Paston's bailiff advised her to stock up with herrings for the winter while they were cheap:

Mistress, it were good to remember your stuff of herring now this fishing time. I have got me a friend in Lowestoft to help buy me seven or eight barrels and they shall not cost more than 6s 8d a barrel. You shall do more [better] now [autumn] with 40s [£2] than you shall do at Christmas with 5 marks [worth over £3].

Although she was by no means poor, a housewife like Margaret Paston had to look for the lowest prices when it came to buying expensive imported items such as spices, as this request to her husband shows:

I send you 5s to buy with sugar and dates for me. I would have 3 or 4 lb of sugar and send me word what price a pound of pepper, cloves, mace, ginger, cinamon, almonds, rice, raisins of currants, galingale, saffron, grains and comfits – of each of these send me word what a pound is worth, and if it be better cheap at London than it is here, I shall send you money to buy such stuff as I will have.   *Paston Letters*

Although there were plenty of servants to do the work, they had to be supervised. Like a modern farm manager, the medieval lady had to see that the crops were raised and animals tended properly, and this meant understanding all about them. One medieval lord wrote a book of advice for his wife, and this extract illustrates the kinds of things she was expected to do:

Let her go often into the fields to see how they are working...and let her make them get up in the morning. If she be a good housewife, let her rise herself, throw on a houppelande [gown], and go to the window and shout until she sees

Making medicines and watching over the sick was a very important part of women's responsibilities. From a Flemish manuscript, 15th century.

them come running out, for they are given to laziness...When you are in the country...order those whose business it is to take thought for the beasts. You likewise ought to show your folk that you know about it all and care about it, for so they will be the more diligent.

The Goodman of Paris, 1393

Social duties

The upper-class lady did the kinds of work done by community workers and health visitors today. Since doctors and surgeons were few and far between and only called upon for serious illness and operations, the lady of the

11

manor, rather like a local nurse, often looked after the sick. She might dress wounds, deliver babies, help with accidents, supply medicines and herbal remedies. Here Margaret Paston asks her husband to send some medicinal syrup which she called treacle. She needed it to treat a young man in the neighbourhood.

Right worshipful husband, I recommend one to you, desiring heartily to hear of your welfare... I pray you heartily that ye will send me a pot with treacle in haste, for I have been right evil at ease and your daughter both since ye yeden [went] hence, and one of the tallest young men of this parish lyeth sick, and hath a great myrr [catarrh] – how he shall do God knoweth. I have sent my Uncle Berney the pot with treacle that ye did buy for him...   *Paston Letters*

An important part of medical care, which may not seem so important today, was watching over the sick. Many illnesses were not understood or treated as quickly as today and women spent a great deal of time looking after people who had long-lasting diseases. A wealthy woman also visited the poor and gave them money. Often she did such 'good works', as they were called, for the local nunnery.

Her children were taken off her hands; they were looked after by nurses when they were young, and sent to live at the homes of friends or relatives when they were older. This was considered the best way of training young people for adult life. But the lady had to arrange their marriages. She also had to keep an eye on the behaviour of all the people, young and old, who were living in her house – from unruly servants to elderly relatives.

Margaret Paston brought up eight children. The marriage of one of her daughters caused her a great deal of trouble. Without her parents' permission, the girl made secret vows to marry the family's bailiff, who, because he owned no property, was considered an unsuitable match. Her mother tried to prevent the marriage and even went as far as to get the bishop to try to prove the vows unsound. Finally when she was unable to do anything to stop the marriage she turned her daughter out of the house and never forgave her.

She enquired after suitable wives for her sons and money was an important issue, as this letter from her son shows:

I heard while I was in London where was a goodly young woman to marry, which was daughter to one Seff, a mercer; and she shall have £200 in money to her marriage and ten marks by the year of land after the death of a stepmother of hers.   *Paston Letters*

However, it also seems that money was not considered to be the only thing to think about in marriage. This letter written in 1476, is from Dame Elizabeth Brew whose daughter was to be engaged to Margaret Paston's son John. Clearly she thought that her daughter's worth could not be measured by her dowry:

And Cousin, that day that she is married, my father will give her 50 marks. But and we accord [agree], I shall give you a greater treasure, that is a witty gentlewoman, and, if I say it, both good and virtuous; for if I should take money for her, I would not give her for a £1,000.

A lady also cared about the marriages of her servants and employees. Margaret Paston seems to have been very concerned that Jane, one of her servants, should not be heart broken:

I would ye should speak with Wykes [a servant] and know his disposition [feelings] to Jane. She hath said, since he departed hence, but [unless] she might have him she would never [be] married; her heart is sore set on him. She told me that he said to her that there was no woman in the world he loved so well. I would not that he should jape [deceive] her...   *Paston Letters*

Independent women

Although most wealthy women were married by about the age of fourteen, many women led a greater part of their lives independently of men. Many married women were widowed, some two or three times, due to their husbands dying in wars. Women without husbands could and did own their own land. Married women could make their own wills and these tell us that they had their own goods and their own friends and social lives.

This rich thirteenth-century widow for example, owned a lot of land. When her will was drawn up, Alice de Beaufow, widow of Thomas de Beaufow, was twenty and had one two-year-old son as heir.

12

Her land in Seaton is worth £5 6s 8d with this stock, namely two ploughs, a hundred sheep, two draught animals, five sows, one boar and four cows. In the first year in which the land has been in her hand she has received in rent 36 shillings and ten pence [36s 10d] and two pounds of pepper, and apart from the rent her tenants have given her 4 shillings [4s] and three loads of oats. *From the will of Alice de Beaufow*

From the wills made by rich women we find that they owned a good deal in the way of personal and household items. Christina of Long Bennington in Lincolnshire, a widow, left a list of her goods in her will in 1283. This is what she owned:

A mare, 2 cows, a horse, 2 oxen, 5 pigs, 120 sheep, a farm cart and stores of grain. A chest, a caldron, bran pot, 2 small pots, 2 posettes [jugs], 2 pans, 1 basin, 1 wash bowl, 6 carpets, 14 linen sheets, 3 pillows, 3 blankets, a coverlet, a feather bed, 12 yards of linen cloth, 4 leaden vessels, 2 napkins, 2 towels. A blue trimmed gown, a shirt, a frock, a gown, a cloak, a headress and a tunic

From the will of Christina de Long Bennington

She also left £7 in silver pennies, which went to the local church, the sick, lepers and orphans.

The wide influence that women from the wealthy classes had is shown by the way they often provided for local people in their wills. Money was left to the sick and poor, servants and tenants, religious organisations and charity, and even for repairing roads and bridges. These extracts are from the will of Lady Alice West of Hampshire, made in 1395:

Also I leave £40 to be distributed among all my servants, men and women of my household, to those who have looked after Thomas, my son, and me and I wish it to be distributed fairly to every man and woman according to their position. Also I leave £40 to be distributed among my poor tenants on all my land, that is to say, to those who are in the greatest need. Also I leave to Elizabeth Rogers, wife of Newe, who was once my servant, 100 shillings [£5]...Also I leave to Richard Forstrer, who is a blind man living in Hanefield who was once a servant of my husband, Sir Thomas West, 20 marks...Also I leave to John Smart who was once my husband's bailiff, 100 shillings.

Lady Peryne Clanbowe, who made her will in 1422, left £10 for the public work of mending bridges and bad roads:

Also I bequeth, to cloth wyth if poormen £20. Also I bequeth to amende brygges and foule wayes £10.

This is just some of the evidence about women from the upper classes in the Middle Ages. It tells us that they played a very active part in society – just as active as men, even though officially they did not have the same rights. We get a very different picture by looking at what the women themselves wrote, thought, and did, rather than at what men thought they should be doing and thinking. But what about women in other classes of society?

Artist painting self-portrait on panel. From Boccaccio,
Le livre des femmes nobles et renommées,
French manuscript, 15th century.

Cy apres senluit de saphe lesbie poe
terrelle t güt clergesse la xlbij i:

aphe lesbie si
fut vne pucel
le de la cite et
de la ville de
mitene et
nauons plus
cougnoussance de tout son h
gnage fors delle. Bien
est verite se nous voulous pe

A lady teaching. From Boccaccio, Le livre des femmes nobles et renommées, *French manuscript, 15th century.*

4 The nun in the convent

Entering the convent

Religion was an important force in the Middle Ages and everyone went to church on Sundays; they were fined if they did not. Women who wished to devote their lives to religion went into nunneries. Others became nuns because it was the only respectable alternative to marriage for an upper-class lady and could represent a good career for her. Some women became nuns unwillingly. Occasionally a young girl was sent to a convent by her relatives who then took over the wealth she had inherited.

Convents varied considerably in size and wealth. Most nunneries were small and struggled to make ends meet. In some of the poorer houses in the north of England nuns even went short of food. Only a few convents such as Barking and Syon in the south of England were rich and influential.

Even so, nuns came from wealthy and noble homes, since novices had to pay a dowry to be accepted. In large families it was common for one or two daughters to become nuns because the dowry paid to a convent would be less than that of a marriage settlement. Robert de Playce in 1345 left money for his niece to go into a convent:

I bequesth to the daughter of John de Playce, my brother 100s in silver, for an aid towards making her a nun ine one of the houses of Wickham, Yedingham or Muncton.

The will of Robert de Playce

In addition to the dowry a novice had to bring with her a habit, a bed and other furniture. One novice in the fourteenth century at Shepey brought in a feather bed, complete with bed linen, furniture and kitchen equipment to make her life more comfortable.

On entering a convent a young girl had her head shorn and was given special clothes to wear. This was a sign that the nun had given up worldly values and fashion in favour of spiritual life. From an Italian manuscript, late 15th century.

Nuns in choir. Which nun is not paying attention? From a French manuscript, 15th century.

A fehterbed, a bolster, ij[2] pyllowys, a payre of blankatts, ij[2] corse coverleds, iiij[4] pare of sheets good and badde,...a lytill brasse pot, a cawydyron and drynkyng pot of pewter.
Dame Agnes Browne's Chamber,Isle of Shepey

To enter a convent was an expensive business which most ordinary people could not afford. Peasants did not wish to get rid of their daughters by sending them to nunneries because they were useful working in the fields, spinning or brewing at home.

Religious services

In most convents the nuns were expected to keep a balance between prayer, study and work. Religion obviously played an important role and prayer gave shape to the day. Each nun had seven services to say each day. The first service began at 2am and the nuns got out of bed and went down in the dark and cold to attend Matins, followed by Lauds. After the services they returned to bed and slept for

about three hours until 6 am. Throughout the rest of the day they attended the services of Prime, Tierce, Sext, None, Vespers, ending with Compline at 7 or 8 pm after which they were supposed to go straight to bed.

However, because girls and women did not always enter the convent for religious reasons, some did not take the services seriously, especially in the later Middle Ages. Nuns often came late to Matins because they had sat up drinking, and talking after Compline. At the priory at Stainfield sometimes half an hour went by between the last stroke of the Matin bell and the beginning of the service. Many nuns slept through the services because they were so tired. The most usual fault was to say the service as quickly as possible. Nuns left the syllables out at the beginning and end of words, skipped sentences and mumbled or slurred their words. At Catesby in 1442, Isabel Benet said:

divine service is chanted at so great a speed that no pauses are made.

Some nuns took their pets into the service even though it was strictly forbidden. At ordinary church services people brought in animals too; there were gentlemen with hawks on their wrists and ladies with dogs. Dogs were also the favourite pets of nuns, but monkeys, squirrels, rabbits and birds were also kept. William of Wykeham, who was Bishop of Winchester said:

We have convinced ourselves by clear proof that some of the nuns of your house bring with them to church, birds, rabbits, hounds, and such like frivolous things…and give more heed (to them) than to the offices of the church…to the grevious peril of their souls, therefore we strictly forbid you all…to bring to church, no birds, hounds, rabbits or other frivolous things.

Romsey, 1387

Services must sometimes have been very noisy with all these animals.

Meal times

Each nun had three meals a day. Breakfast consisted of bread and ale. Nuns usually had a weekly allowance of seven loaves of bread and a good supply of beer. Sometimes they had to drink water instead of ale. The nuns preferred ale and complained about having to do without their alcohol. At midday, as part of a big meal the nuns ate beef, pork or bacon on meat days and fresh or salt fish on fish days. During fast periods like Lent when meat was not allowed, the nuns ate dried or salt fish with dried peas, almonds, raisins or figs. For supper the nuns had a light meal of fish or white meat which was easy to digest.

For supper sche schall ordeyn for some lytel sowpyng [soup], and for syche [fish] and shyte [white] mete or for any other thynge lyghte of dygestyon and as gode to the bodyly helthe.

Syon, 1536

In many convents nuns were not allowed to speak to each other even at meal times. They used sign language if they wanted the salt passed, or more helpings of food and drink. At Syon in 1536 the nuns had 106 different signs. A nun would:

'Wagge her hande displaied sidelynges in manner of a fissch tail'

if she wanted fish.

'Draw her left little fynger in manner of mylkyng'

if she wanted milk,

'Hold her nose in the uppere parte of her righte fiste and rubbe it'

if she wanted mustard.

Nuns were told that they should only use sign language if it was absolutely necessary. This is not surprising if we think of the laughter that some of these must have caused and the fun that meal times could be.

A less serious aspect of convent life. From a Flemish manuscript, 14th century.

Work in the convent

Life was busy in the convents. They were not just religious houses devoted to prayer and the worship of God, but were self-sufficient communities. All nuns were expected to work for about five hours a day. Some had specific jobs to do, but many were involved in the general work of the convent such as haymaking, digging and spinning.

At the head of each convent was the abbess or prioress, who was responsible for discipline and order in the nunnery. If the abbess was efficient, the nuns in a richer convent were well provided for, but if she was a poor manageress the nuns were ill-fed and badly-dressed.

Particular nuns were in charge of the religious side of the convent, such as the chantress who trained the nuns to sing nicely, and the sacrist who was in charge of preparing everything for the church. The sacrist ensured that the altar cloths and vestments were kept in good, clean condition and the plate for the services in order. She also bought the wax, tallow and wicks to make the church candles.

18   *Nuns in the refectory. Manuscript from Florence, 14th century.*

There were other nuns in charge of household management, servants, the accounts and management of all the properties. A nun called the fractress took care of all the eating arrangements; she kept the chairs and tables in repair, purchased the dishes and table cloths, and made sure the tables were laid properly and that the lavatories were kept clean. A cellaress made sure the nuns had enough to eat and ordered all the necessary items.

The celeres schall purvey for [buy] mete and drynke, ordenying for alle...in the bakhows, brewhows, kychen, buttry, pantry, celer and suche other. *Syon*

Most of the food was grown on the home farm which was attached to the convent. Anything which the farm could not produce had to be brought, such as salt, dried fish and spices, which was usually obtained from the village market. At Syon in 1536, the nuns bought for their year's supply:

749¾lbs sugar	18lbs Nutmeg
500lbs Almonds	4lbs Currants
6lbs Ginger	6lbs Pepper
111lbs Cloves	111lbs Cinnamon.
3 qrs Rice	

The nun in charge ordered the meals, made sure that the servants worked hard and kept an account of all that was spent.

This nun is using a distaff to spin wool for the convent. From a French manuscript, 13th to 14th century.

An infirmaress saw to all the needs of the sick, changed their bed linen, administered medicine and fed them. Nuns were possibly skilled in herbal medicines and in the more simple forms of home medicine like bleeding, just like any lady of the day. Doctors were only called for more serious illnesses. An infirmaress would:

Change ther beddes and clothes, geve them medycecynes, ley to ther plastres and mynyster to them mete and drynke, fyre and water nyghte and day.

She had to be considerate and kind with people who were sick and had to make sure they were made as comfortable as possible.

Not squames [squeamish] to wasche them, and sype them, nor noyde them, not angry nor hasty, nor unpacient thof one have the vomit. *Syon*

All of these women had to keep careful accounts of the money they spent. Each year they gave their accounts to the treasuress who was responsible for the general financial management of the nunnery. If all these women ran their affairs well convent life could be comfortable and pleasurable in one of the larger nunneries. In some of the poorer convents, though, the nuns had desperately little to live on and were continually in financial difficulties, in spite of all of their efforts.

Education

It was on the continent that convents mainly became centres of learning and scholarship. St Hildegard of Bingen in Germany was a clever and famous nun, who many believed to be a prophet. She wrote books about science and philosophy as well as religion. Hildegard had visions which even the Pope, the head of the Roman Catholic Church, respected. He wrote in admiration to Hildegard, praising her religious understanding.

We are filled with admiration, my daughter for the new miracles that God has shown you, filling you with his spirit so that you see, understand and communicate many secret things. Reliable persons who have seen and heard you vouch for these facts.
Pope Eugenius, 1148

A nun at prayer. From a French manuscript around the 15th century.

However in England (certainly towards the end of the Middle Ages) most nuns were educated to the same standard as noble ladies of the time. Although they were supposed to be able to read and understand Latin and French not all could do so. All the same, many great lords, country gentlemen and wealthy merchants sent their children to convents to be educated.

Nuns and the outside world

Although most nunneries had less than thirty nuns living in them, the abbesses of larger convents had similar responsibilities to a lord of the manor. The abbess in these ranked amongst the great people of the country, enjoyed the same position and received the same dues and loyalty as a great lord. Many people depended on her for employment and assistance in times of stress.

Whereas in the poorer convents nuns had to do their own cooking and housework, the wealthier ones had a regular staff of ordinary

people to assist them in their daily routine. The larger houses employed a cook, a butler, housekeeper, a malster, to make malt, a brewer and baker to prepare the weekly ration of bread and ale. There were servants to help with the household chores and making of cloth. In some convents nuns had their own personal servants. The Abbess of Barking even employed her own kitchen staff and gentlewoman.

Attached to each convent was a home farm, which provided the nuns with most of their bread, meat, beer, vegetables and dairy produce. Farm labourers were used to plough, sow and harvest and to look after the animals and to help in a dairy. Extra help was needed at harvest time. Harvest workers were normally well fed by the convent on beef, mutton, fish and beer. Many nunneries also gave a goose to workers at the end of the harvest. The nuns of St Michael entered it in their accounts as:

the expenses of the sichel [harvest] goose.

Some of the larger convents had estates all over England. They owned several manors which were either leased to tenants or put in the charge of bailiffs. To keep these estates in good repair the nuns employed thatchers, plumbers, builders and carpenters. The accounts of St Radegunds in 1449 show the convent expenses:

For the hire of John Scot, thatcher, hired to roof with straw the tenement, for 2 days taking 4d a day, at the board of the Lady Prioress 4s...and in the hire of Katherine Rolf for the work of assistant for 12 days at 1½d a day 18d.

The Abbess Euphemia of Wherwell made many improvements to the convent estates. Some of these included the building of a new hall, levelling the court of the abbey manor, rebuilding a new bell tower and presbytery. She built an infirmary for the ailing nuns, a comfortable hygienic dwelling which must have been a pleasant place to convalesce.

Built for the use of both sick and sound, a new and larger farmery away from the main building. Beneath the farmery she constructed a water course, through which a stream flowed with sufficient force to carry of all refuse that might corrupt the air...and...made gardens and vineyards and shrubberies in places that were formerly useless and barren.   *Wherwell, 1226*

One important aspect of work in a nunnery was caring for the sick. Nuns often provided the only hospital care in the area. In the Livre de la vie active des religieuses de l'Hôtel-Dieu, *French, 15th century.*

In the parish of Sheppey the convent employed the whole village. Twenty-six men and seven women worked in the house or on the home farm. The convent employed three shepherds, a cowherd and a horsekeeper. All the other men and women looked after the rest of the animals and crops, or worked in the bakehouse or brewery or dairy. Some of the people employed were:

Mr White, taking 26s 8d by the yere and lyvere [clothing]. John Colls, Butler, lyvere. 26s 7½d. The cowherd by yere 30s and no lyvere. Robard Welshe, brewer, by yere 20s, [£1] no lyvere.

People in their parishes depended financially on the nuns in hard times, for the giving of alms was an important part of their work. On some feast days convents gave herrings, cheese and bread to the poor. At the Great Abbey of Lacock, the nuns recorded:

We ought to feed on All Soul's day as many as there are ladies, to each poor person a dry loaf and as a relish two herrings or a slice of cheese.

Houses often held a part of their property on condition that they gave alms. The abbey at Dartford had to give £5 12 8d twice a week to thirteen poor people.

Convents also acted as hotels for widows and other gentlewomen whose husbands were at war. These women were felt to be safe inside a convent and their financial contribution was a welcome addition to poorer nunneries. Many of these visitors however brought their worldly ways into the convent and encouraged nuns to be more fashion conscious.

21

This is the character Madame Eglentyne, in Chaucer's poem Canterbury Tales, *written in the 14th century. What rule is she disobeying?*

Although jewellery had been strictly forbidden by the church in 1222, many nuns broke this rule:

We decree that nuns…shall not wear a silken wimple, nor dare to carry silver or golden pins in their veil. Neither shall they, wear belts of silk or adorned with gold or silver…and let none but a consecrated nun wear a ring and let her be content with one alone.

According to a visiting bishop in 1441 the Prioress at Ankerwyke wore:

Golden rings exceedingly costly with precious stones and also girdles silvered and silken veils, and she wears furs, round her neck a long cord of silk, hanging below her breast and on it a gold ring with one diamond.

Being a nun did not mean a withdrawal from ordinary everyday life, but a means by which wealthier women could lead a useful and fulfilling existence. It was a career and livelihood for wealthier ladies who were restricted by birth from the choices open to peasant women.

5 Women at work

As with the lady of the manor and the nun during the Middle Ages, ordinary women's lives were far from leisurely. Not only did they have to care for their husbands, their homes and their children, but they also had to work to contribute to the family income.

Countrywomen

The lives of women living in the country could be very harsh as the following extract from William Langland's narrative poem *Piers Plowman*, written between the years 1362 and 1399, tried to point out. Not only were they weighed down caring for the children, but they also had to pay the rent and feed the family, which they tried to do from the money earned from spinning:

Charged with children and overcharged by
  landlords
What they may spare in spinning, they spend on
  rental
On milk or on meal to make porridge
To still the sobbing of the children at meal times.

Women and their families often suffered from hunger, but this was no excuse for not fulfilling all their duties:

Also themselves suffer much hunger
And woe in wintertime, with waking at night
To rise to the [bedside] to rock the cradle...

This woman is using a loom to weave woollen cloth. From an English manuscript, 14th century.

In this picture one woman is spinning and the other is carding (preparing the wool). From an English manuscript, 14th century.

24   *Haymaking in June. From* Les très riches heures du duc de Berry, *French, 15th century.*

Both to card [prepare wool for spinning], and to
Comb [comb wool for spinning], to clout
 [mend]
And to wash, to rub, and to reel [wind]
And rushes to peel [for rush lights].

William Langland thought it too sad to write
about. He said:

The woe of these women who dwell in hovels
Is too sad to speak of or to say in rhyme.
Piers Plowman

Peasant women had a varied workload.
They had to make all the family's food and
clothes from raw materials. There were no
ready-made foods or clothes shops. Outside the
house they milked the cows, and combed out
flax. They were responsible for feeding the
chickens, ducks and geese, shearing the sheep,
making cheese and looking after the family
vegetable patch. To earn extra money they
spun and wove, and sold the cloth. They
certainly had no time to spare, and as you can
see in the picture often when they went out to
help their husbands, they took their spinning
with them.

They also worked with their husbands in the
fields: sowing, reaping, gleaning, binding,
threshing and winnowing. At times, they even
helped with the hardest job of all which was
ploughing.

Unmarried countrywomen

Girls who did not marry might decide to
remain on their father's land, and work for
him or their brothers in return for food and
lodging. They might decide to become servants
in another peasant's home, where they received
food and clothes in return for their labours.
Some girls chose to go and work for the lord of
the manor as dairy assistants, or brewers of ale.
Others hired themselves out as labourers and
did the same work as men – haymaking,
thatching, weeding, sowing, reaping and
binding.

Often they travelled around the country in
search of work, but they first had to obtain
permission from the lord of the manor to leave
the village where they lived. Both men and

This couple are collecting nuts to feed the pigs. The wife has brought her spinning with her. From the Book of Hours *produced in Rouen in the 1480s.*

25

This couple are working in the field. What job are they doing? From the Book of Hours *produced in Rouen in the 1480s.*

women were tied to the land they worked. If they managed to escape and stay free for a year and a day, they could keep their freedom.

Widows

If widows inherited their husbands' lands they might decide to hand the lands on to their sons, who then had to look after their mothers. Some widows decided to keep the land themselves. If they did this, they not only had to farm the land and look after the livestock, but they also had to fulfil their duties to their lord, this included giving him a share of whatever they produced. Otherwise, they were fined or even lost their lands. Here are some examples of widows being fined for neglecting their duties. In 1299 a widow named Alice Alte Dame got into trouble for not repairing her house and outbuildings. At Tooting in 1246 Maud, widow of Robin, and Mabel, widow of Spendelowe, were fined 6d each for encroaching on the lord's land. In 1247, Lucy Rede was in court because her cattle had strayed onto the lord's pasture.

In this extract from the *Nun's Priest's Tale* written in the 1380s, Chaucer described a widow who led a very simple but not uncomfortable life:

Thre large sowes [pigs] hadde she, and namo,
Three keen [cows], and eek a sheep that hight
    Malle. [is called Molly].
Full sooty was hire bour and eke hir halle,
In which she eet ful many a sklendre meel.
Canterbury Tales

Her diet kept her in good health we are told, and consisted of milk, bacon and an egg.

Hir bord was served moost with with and blak, –
Milk and broun breed, in which she foond no
    lak,
Seynd [broiled] bacoun and somtime an ey
    [egg] or tweye;
For she was, as it were a maner deye. [kind of
    dairymaid]   *Canterbury Tales*

Although their lives were hard, and they worked as a means of survival, there may often have been some truth in this statement by Christine de Pisan who felt that peasant women's lives were more secure than those of

In this picture the hay is being cut. What would it be used for? From the Book of Hours, *Rouen, 1480s.*

Here they are killing a pig and collecting the blood. What might the blood be used for? From the Book of Hours, *Rouen, 1480s.*

27

What different jobs can you see being done by countrywomen in these pictures? These are all from Flemish manuscripts of the 14th and 15th centuries.

the upper classes. Peasant women may also have enjoyed greater equality.

'Albeit [Though] they be fed with coarse bread, milk lard, and pottage [soup] and drink water, and albeit they have care and labour enow [enough], yet is their life surer [securer] yea they have greater sufficiency [are more able to look after themselves] than some that be of higher estate.'   *Christine de Pisan*

28

Townswomen

Many women, particularly those in the towns, went to learn a trade or skill. To do this they had to serve an apprenticeship. An apprenticeship meant that they lived with a family for an agreed number of years, usually seven. During that time the husband or wife taught them a trade. The agreement, which was a legal document, made between the two families was called an indenture. The following is an extract from John Nougle of London agreeing to his sister Katherine becoming apprenticed to Avice Wodeford in 1392.

This indenture witnesses that John Nougle of London, haberdasher [someone who makes ribbons, tape etc.], has put Katherine Nougle his sister apprentice to Avice Wodeford, silkthrower [someone who twists silk into thread], of London to learn her art and to serve her after the manner of an apprentice from Pentecost [Whit Sunday] in the 15th year of the reign of King Richard II until the end of the next sevrne yeares...
Indenture of Katherine Nougle to Avice Wodeford

Tradeswomen

Whereas, by an act of parliament in 1363, men had to keep to one trade, women were allowed to change between different ones during their working lives. Many trades done by women were not particularly skilled; such as that of a flaunor who made flauns, a sort of pancake. Women were also herb wives and sellers of old clothes. They sold fish which was a profitable business, since there were many fast days, (e.g. Friday) on which the Church forbade people to eat meat. Another popular trade for women was selling poultry.

Women were also employed in the more skilled trades such as, mercers (dealers in fabrics), drapers (sellers of cloth), grocers and merchants. Sometimes they even served the King: Mariot de Ferars, for example, sold saddles, horses and harnesses to Henry III, who paid £75 for the goods; Dynoisia la Roura was responsible for providing wheels for the King's visit to Scotland in 1301.

Sewing, embroidery, washing and acting as midwives were always considered women's work. Women, however, were also found in the following trades which may be thought of as men's work. There were women barbers, apothecaries (chemists), armourers (makers of armour), shipwrights, blacksmiths and tailors. Some painted and one particular woman artist must have been quite talented as she had an apprentice. In her will she left this apprentice one-third of her materials and a chest to keep them in. Apprentices quite often benefited in this way.

In nearly all trades there were fewer women than men. For example in London in 1420, only 20 out of 300 brewers were female. One reason for this was that women often gave up their apprenticeship because they got married. The possibility of marriage was considered in the indenture. Normally women could either

A woman pedlar. From an English manuscript, 14th century.

A woman blacksmith. From an English manuscript, 14th century.

29

continue the apprenticeship or pay a fee to be released. In the indenture of Katherine Nougle it said:

...Nor should she contract matrimony, [get married] with any man during her said term save, [except] with the assent, [agreement] and will and counsel [advice] of the said John and Thomas Nougle, citizen and tailor, of London, uncle of the same apprentice.

In 1376, the indenture of Agnes Cok stated that:

...If the said Agnes wished to take a husband, she might choose either to serve the rest of her term, or to pay the sum of 4 marks.

Women who completed their apprenticeship often ended up with large and profitable businesses. A certain Alice de Canterbrugge had £200 worth of armour and other goods stolen from her; and the Earl of Lincoln bought a piece of embroidered cloth from Aleyce Day and Thomasina Guidydichon for 300 marks – a lot of money in those days.

Most silkworkers were women. They made fringes, tassels, ribbons, lace and girdles. They were a powerful group. In 1468 they complained to the King about a man called Nicholas Sardouche who was buying up all the available silk and selling it to them at higher prices:

Nicholas Sardouche for a long time past has been in the habit of forestalling and regrating [reselling] all the crude and coloured silk and other kind of merchandise brought by aliens [foreigners], thus greviously enhancing [pushing up] the price, as was openly proved by his confession before the mayor and aldermen, [councillors] that he had recently brought all the silk he could find in the City and raised the price by 4/- [4s].

Women employers

Both men and women took on apprentices of both sexes. Here is one example from the fifteenth century:

John de Staundone, cornmonger, admitted to the freedom of the City for that he had been apprenticed of Agnes d'Evre, wife of John de Coventerl, cornmonger.

Often the apprentices were tiresome, but their masters and mistresses were not supposed to ill-treat them.

This is a woman shopkeeper. What is she selling? From the Hours of the Virgin, *Flanders, 16th century.*

30

Sureties [guarantees] were accepted for Agnes, wife of John Cotiller, that she would instruct her apprentice Juseana in proper manner, would find her food and drink and would not beat her with stick or knife.   *1364*

This was not always followed, and sometimes they were badly treated.

John Carter of Reading brought a bill of complaint against Ellis Mympe, bouderer [embroider] of London, to whom his daughter Alice had been apprenticed of for five years, beating and ill-treating the girl and failing to provide for her.   *1369*

Often strict rules on behaviour were laid down for the apprentice. In the case of Katherine Nougle:

...She should not commit fornication or adultery in the house of her said mistress or without during the said term, nor play any unlawful games, whereby her mistress may have any loss. She shall not customarily visit a tavern, save to do the business of the said mistress...

When an apprentice had completed her training she could take up her trade. On 8 September, 1311, Agnes La Blake became a qualified brewster.

'Femme sole'

This term, was used to describe women who traded on their own. Sometimes this was because they were single or widowed:

Widows of London who make great trade in wool, and other things, as Isabella Buckerall and others.

Sometimes they were married women who went on with their jobs, after marriage, and carried on a trade, separate from their husbands. If they became involved in a legal dispute their husbands were not responsible for their debts. This is made quite clear in the Lincoln rule, and other large cities had similar rules.

If any woman that has a husband use any craft within the city, whereof her husband meddles not, she shall be charged as a sole woman as touching such things as belongeth to her craft. And if a plaint [complaint] be taken against such a woman she shall answer and pleed as a sole woman and make her law and take other advantage in court by plea or otherwise for her

discharge. And if she be condemned she shall be committed to prison till she be agreed with the plaintiff, and no goods or chattels that belongeth to her husband shall be confiscated.

'Femmes sole' were also responsible for chasing up their own debts. Around 1300, when Mabel, the wife of John le Heymugger was not paid for some beer she had sold, it was up to her to recover the debt.

The plaintiff said she took the beer without her husband's knowledge and that she kept an inn, received guests and traded sole.

When husbands and wives were in business together then the husband was responsible for his wife's debts and misdeeds. In 1327 there was an interesting case in which ten bakers were found guilty of stealing dough. Two of the culprits were married women who traded with their husbands. The eight men were put in the pillory, but the women were not punished because the deed was not theirs in the eyes of the law.

Guilds

Each trade or craft had its own guild which protected the interests of the members. The guild looked after them in times of need, providing such things as sickness benefit, or the money for a funeral. There is no evidence to suggest that women had separate organisations, but it is difficult to say whether they enjoyed the same position as men in the guilds. They may only have been admitted because they were the wives or sisters of members, but there is at least one reference to suggest that they might have received the same benefits as men. In 1414, the Merchant Taylors built almshouses:

For their poor brethren and sisters.

The part women played in the economy of the Middle Ages was considerable. As a result of this, they too, like men, often adopted as their surname the trade or occupation they followed – brewster, webster, baxter, kempster, laundress, fisher, flesher. As well as leading busy and industrious lives, however, some women came up against the law, as the next chapter will show.

6 Women law-breakers

Most descriptions of law and order in the Middle Ages give the impression that women did not break the law. They might occasionally be corrected for nagging their men-folk, generally their husbands, and for this they were punished by being forced to wear a scold's bridle which was like a dog's muzzle and stopped them talking. They were also put in a ducking stool and ducked in the river.

These were minor offences, but there is evidence to show that women's part in law-breaking was much more serious.

In this chapter, you will see some examples of the types of crime committed by women, as well as the kind of behaviour that was considered to be unacceptable in the Middle Ages. Women's involvement in crime was often different from men's. Some of their actions are

Women prisoners being brought before the Seneschal (administrator) of Hainault (a province now in Belgium). What evidence is there in this picture which suggests that these women are wealthy? From a French manuscript, early 15th century.

particularly female forms of law-breaking, so it is important to understand why they committed crimes and why they acted in a way which caused people to turn against them and to punish them.

Women criminals

There were fewer women than men criminals in the Middle Ages, just as there are today. In the thirteenth and fourteenth centuries, about 10% of the names written in the court records are women's. In the majority of cases mentioned, the women involved in crime were working with other members of their family.

For example, in 1332, Alice le French, along with her husband and a friend, robbed and murdered a foreign Hospitaller on the King's highway and stole ten silver marks from him.

Margery of Sibbertoft was arrested for divers (various) thefts and taken to the gaol in Northampton Castle and handed to John Douel, the Sheriff, 26 Edward I [i.e. the 26th year of his reign–1298]. She escaped...and took sanctuary in the church of St. Mary in Northampton, but afterwards surrendered herself to trial.

Margery was tried by the judge and her case was recorded. It is only through these court records that we know about Margery.

Most peasants did not need to know how to

This picture, of a woman stealing, is from a manuscript which illustrates the seven deadly sins. What is the woman stealing? From a French manuscript, late 14th century.

read and write, so their lives were only recorded when they came into contact with officials; breaking the law was such an occasion. All the courts kept careful records of the cases before them. These tell us not only what the person was suspected of, but they also give us a glimpse of their everyday lives. The cases allow us to see what sort of behaviour and life-style was considered to be acceptable in the Middle Ages.

In some cases, as in that case of Agnes and Maud Pikhorn, the records say that women organised the crime. Neighbours swore that they organised an attack on a family which they then tried to cover up.

At twilight on 23 April 1271, felons and thieves came to the house of John Reyd of Ravensden while John, his wife Maud and servants, Walter Astwood, and Richard Pikhorn, were sitting at supper. They entered the door towards the courtyard on the west side and immediately assaulted John, striking him on the head near the crown with an axe, and to the heart with a knife, of which he immediately died. They wounded Maud on the right side of the head, almost cut off her left hand, and heated a trivet and placed her upon it so they left her almost dead. Walter and Richard were tied up and all the goods of the house were robbed and carried away. *Bedfordshire Coroner's Rolls*

When women were brought to trial along with their husbands and relatives, the courts spent a lot of time making sure that the women had not been forced into taking part in the crime by their husbands or brothers. In this case, Isabel, the daughter of Stacie of Rudham, was on trial for helping her husband and others to steal:

two marks of silver and other goods to the value of forty shillings. And also for plundering by robbery the chaplain of the church of Fornsett of his goods and chattels, to the value of sixty shillings.

The jury had to make certain that Isabel had decided of her own free will, to help with the robberies.

And of the forsaid Isabel they say that she is the wife of the forsaid Simon Brid but they say that she was present together with the forsaid Simon her husband and the other forsaid thieves at the two robberies committed at Hertfordebrigge and at the robbery committed at Manegrene. And the jurors having been asked if the forsaid Isabel had been at any robbery or theft in the absence of Simon her husband say on their oath that she was not. Asked further if she had been compelled by her husband to be present at the robberies they say that she was not but that she accompanied Simon her husband, and the other thieves, without the coercion of her husband, to those robberies. And they say that the same Simon was present with Isabel when the robberies were committed. Therefore regarding judgement to be given on the forsaid Isabel, the court adjourns to consider. Meanwhile Isabel is to stay in prison in the custody of Thomas de Hyndringham, sheriff. *Justices Itinerant Rolls*

All the other people involved in this robbery were hung.

Burglary and theft

Men and women did the same work on the land, but inside the home it was a different matter. The women cooked the meals, made the clothes and nursed the baby. It is not surprising then that when women committed a crime, it was connected to their interests in the home and with their family.

In the early fourteenth century, women played a larger part in receiving and counterfeiting than any other crime. The court records do not give any reasons for this.

The most common crime among women was burglary and theft. When women stole, they stole things which they could use in their homes: clothing and household goods. Often they stole food. In 1321 Agnes Weldon, together with three of her children was accused of stealing sheaves worth 4d. Grain, bread, cheese, fish and meat made up one-third of the goods women stole, but only one-eighth of what men stole. In the Great Famine of 1315–17, the percentage of women involved in crime went up. When food became easily available again after 1325, the number of women criminals went down.

Violent crimes

In the Middle Ages, the sons of barons and lords of the manor were trained for war. The ability to fight was seen as an essential skill to be taught to all boys. No wonder then that

One case recorded in Bedfordshire tells of a woman who killed her husband as he was lying in bed by cutting his throat with a hatchet and breaking his skull with a billhook (a hatchet used for pruning trees). She sought sanctuary and claimed in her defence that her husband had gone mad and had been 'seized by death'. At a time when divorce was impossible, murder was one way of getting rid of a husband or wife.

Infanticide

It is likely that more women were involved in murder than the cases in the court roll records show. Women appearing before the judge were those who had been caught. There was one crime which women found easy to cover up: infanticide (the killing of young babies). This was one way of keeping the size of the family down at a time when there was no effective contraception. Girl babies were more likely to be killed than boy babies.

There is one gruesome explanation of infanticide which probably has little truth in it: Johannes de Trokebwe, a chronicler, claimed that parents killed off their children in order to eat them during the Great Famine 1315–17.

Before 1623, a mother killing her illegitimate child was in trouble with the Church and not the law courts.

Women who were brought to trial for the murder of children were more often than not found to be mad or ill. In the early fourteenth century Matilde, widow of Mark le Waleys of Bathonwell, tried to commit suicide by throwing herself in the river. She was prevented from doing so by her neighbours, but when she returned home, she murdered all her children. Another case is that of Margaret Calbot who killed her two daughters. Since the jury found her to be insane she was not found guilty and hung, but returned to prison.

The jurors say on oath that Margaret killed with a stick Agnes of the age of two years [when] lying in the cradle and Matilda sister of Agnes in the house of the same Margaret, being of the age of four years sitting near the hearth...But they say that at the time when Margaret committed these felonies and for a long time before and after, she was continually possessed

A woman beating a man with a distaff. What would she normally use this for? From an English manuscript, 14th century.

most of the violent crimes were committed by men.

Of the 2,696 cases of murder tried in the counties of Norfolk, Yorkshire and Northamptonshire at the beginning of the fourteenth century, nine-tenths of the cases involved men. Yet there were women murderers. Their weapons were not the sword and staff of the battlefields, but the knives and hatchets they used for their cooking, or chopping wood, or the distaff they used for spinning wool.

Generally their victims were members of their own families, mainly their husbands and children.

by madness...and she wished to have killed William her husband by day and night...and they say that Margaret was mad at the time when she killed Agnes and Matilda. Therefore she is sent to prison until the will of the lord king should be known.   *Justices Itinerant Rolls*

Punishment of criminals

In the Middle Ages both men and women were hanged if they were found guilty of a crime. When it came to the crime of treason (a crime against the country), then the punishment was different. A man was hung, drawn and quartered, but for the sake of modesty, in order not to expose the lower-part of a woman's body, she was burned at the stake. Women accused of murdering their husbands received a very different punishment from the husbands who murdered their wives. Women were considered to have committed an act of treason because they were expected to obey their husbands, just as husbands were expected to obey the lord of the manor.

In 1326, Lucia, the widow of Thomas Tasseburgh, who killed Thomas in Norwich, was burned for her crime, but her servant was not convicted.

Lucy who was the wife of Thomas de Taseburgh and May servant of the same Lucy [who have been] charged before the king of the death of the said Thomas de Taseburgh who was killed in Norwich in the seventeenth year of the reign of the present king...Lucy and May say they are guilty of nothing...Then the truth is sought...The jurors of the city of Norwich chosen for this say on their oath that the forsaid Lucy is guilty of the death of Thomas formerly

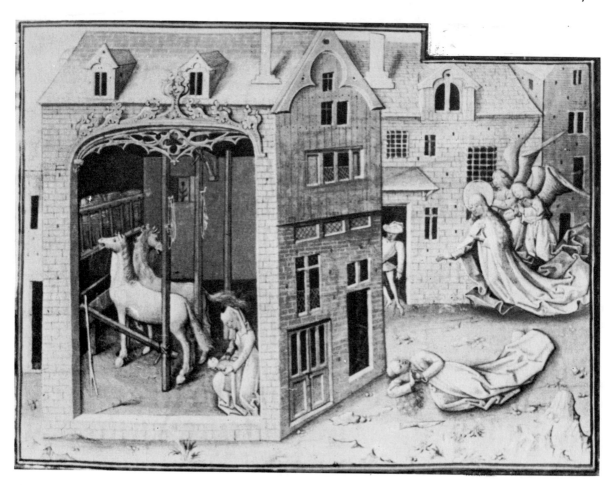

A woman being saved from suicide by the Virgin Mary after killing her baby. Where and how did the woman kill her baby? Why do you think she did this? Find something in the picture which shows you how she intended to kill herself. From a Flemish manuscript, 15th century.

her husband and that the forsaid May is not guilty of the same death. Therefore Lucy is to be burned and May is quit. The forsaid Lucy has no chattels etc. *King's Bench Rolls*

Women who were pregnant when they were convicted were not executed until after the child was born. Such women were examined by a female jury to see if they were telling the truth. If so, they would be returned to prison until the birth of their child. It was sometimes possible for the gaoler to be bribed into allowing a woman to get pregnant.

One woman, Matilda Hereward of Brandiston in Northamptonshire, managed to put off her execution for a year and a half. She appeared before the judge in June 1301 and was found guilty of stealing along with her husband. She was returned to prison because she was pregnant. The same thing happened in September 1301, January 1302, June 1302, October 1302 and in January 1303. Matilda's husband would have been hanged in 1301, so her pregnancies were a result of the mixed prisons. In the fourteenth and fifteenth centuries, more and more English gaols were building separate quarters for women.

The torture of St Margaret, a medieval martyr. Women were not generally hung up by their hair. What is the man to the right of the picture doing? From a French manuscript, early 15th century.

Sanctuary seekers

Another way of avoiding execution which was open to both women and men alike was to seek sanctuary. People accused of a crime had the right to flee to any church or holy ground and confess. Once there, they were safe for forty days. During that time, they had to swear to 'abjure the realm' (banish themselves from England for ever).

Tichmarsh: Margery de Wyreceste took sanctuary in the Church of Our Lady of Tichmarsh, on Wednesday, the Feast of St. Margaret the Virgin [20 July, 1317] and confessed before Henry de Tichness…that she was a common thief and that she had stolen the clothes of John le Matchal at Finedon, viz. two pieces of carpet and two tunics worth together 2s. She abjured the realm and the port of Dover has been assigned to her. She has no chattels.'
Northamptonshire Coroners' Rolls

What happened to Margery, whether she reached the port of Dover and managed to sail from England, we shall never know. There is no record of her after this. According to the laws of the time, Margery was sent from the church at Tichmarsh penniless. She was clothed in sack-cloth and had to carry a white wooden cross in her hand. She had to travel to Dover along the King's highway and was not allowed to spend more than one night in any one place. She was passed from constable to constable and the people in each place where she had to stay overnight had to give her food and shelter.

When she arrived at the port of Dover, if there was no ship ready to sail, the banished Margery would have to go into the sea up to her waist each day. This was to show that she did intend to cross over the sea.

Occasionally, the occupation of the people who sought sanctuary was recorded along with their name and crime. Among the 363 people who took sanctuary between 1275–1329 in Northamptonshire churches, there were four blacksmiths, one of whom was a woman. Muriel le Blacksmith, who took sanctuary during this period, confessed to receiving stolen goods.

A picture from a manuscript of the life of St Margaret, showing St Margaret being thrown into prison. Although this picture illustrates a story, the artist would have based the drawing on everyday sights. From an Italian manuscript, 14th century.

Church courts: judges of behaviour

People's private lives were carefully watched over by the church and it claimed the right to guard people's morals and set up special courts to hear the cases of those who misbehaved.

The Church was particularly concerned with people's sex lives and punished those who had relationships outside marriage. Although both men and women appear before the court on this charge, a more severe attitude was taken towards women than men. Men often ran away, or were not named in court, but women were punished:

The following women have been violated [raped] and therefore must pay the fine for incontinency [having sexual intercourse]. Botild, daughter of Alfred (fine 6d), Margaret, daughter of Hepton (fine 12d), Agnes, daughter of Seaman (fine 2d), Agnes, daughter of Jor (fine 6d), Margot, daughter of Edith (fine 6d).
Wretham Manor, Norfolk, 1247

The Church courts were called upon to settle marriage disputes. Husbands had the right to punish disobedient wives, but the Church did not approve of wife-beating.

Thomas Lonchad treats his wife badly, beating her with a stick. He appears and admits the charge and is whipped in the usual way round the market. *Droitwich, Worcestershire, 1300*

There are, though, more cases appearing before the Church courts which deal with wives

38

who nagged their husbands than wife-beaters. Women who found it difficult to be obedient to their husbands were not to be tolerated, but a blind eye was often turned on the wife-beater.

Keeping the Sabbath

One of the major concerns of the Church was to make sure everyone attended on Sunday and Holy days. Breaking the Sabbath was the most common case appearing before the Church courts. People were fined for working on the Sabbath as these two cases show:

Jane Ferand of Asmoderby is said to have broken the Sabbath, spynning and cardying on the feast of St. Matthew, and doing other things. She admits the crime and is awarded three whippings   *Ripon, Yorkshire, 1468*

Isabella Hunter and Catherine Pykring admit that they washed their linen on St. Mary Magdalene Day. They are to have two whippings with a handful of flax.   *Durham, 1451*

Witchcraft

The Church fined people if they found them practicing medicine or teaching without a special licence granted by them. Women who were healers were often believed to be witches. To accuse a woman of being a witch was to make her an outcast, someone who would be regarded with suspicion by the rest of the village. In some cases it seems that women were accused of being witches out of a desire for revenge, or because they did not fit in with people's ideas of what was normal behaviour.

We cannot as yet be sure of all the evidence concerning witchcraft in the Middle Ages. It does seem likely that many women suspected of witchcraft suffered punishment at the hands of their neighbours, if not in the courts.

Suggestions for study

Chapter 3

1 What kinds of evidence have been used in this chapter to find out about the lives of upper-class women in the Middle Ages? Do the sources tell us about poor women too? What other kind of evidence might tell us about other women's lives?
2 How useful is the will of Lady Alice West (page 13) to historians?
3 What different information do the wills (pages 12 and 13) give us about women's lives at this time? Use the rest of the information in Chapter 3 to help you with your answer.
4 Read through the wills of Alice de Beaufow and Christina de Long Bennington (page 13) and use other books on life in the Middle Ages to help you decide which were a wealthy woman's most valuable possessions. Why was this? What do rich women leave in their wills today?
5 List all the different types of evidence used in Chapter 3. List all the different types of evidence you might wish to use in researching a topic on the lives of wealthy women in Britain today. What has changed and what has remained the same?
6 Read the views of Christine de Pisan on women on page 6. Why do you think these are different to those views expressed by the church on page 3?
7 Make a list of the questions you would like to ask Margaret Paston about her life as lady of the manor in the fourteenth century.

Chapter 4

1 Make up some sign language which could be used at the dinner table in a convent. (Remember that they are not supposed to make you laugh.)
2 After re-reading the evidence in this chapter, imagine you are a nun in a convent. Write a letter home to your sister, who is married to a lord, telling about your life in the convent.
3 Make up a conversation between two novices. One has entered for religious reasons, the other was sent by her family. Include meal times, religious services, work, general attitudes.

Chapter 5

1 Find a more traditional book about life in the Middle Ages. What does this say about:
   ● the lives of peasant women?
   ● the lives of townswomen?
2 Some of the sources used in this chapter come from stories and poems. What are the strengths and weaknesses of using such sources for historians?
3 Look at the pictures of people at work in this chapter. What sort of energy are people using?
4 Look carefully at the pictures on page 23. Find out what the machines are used for and say how they worked. What were their limitations? What are the machines made of?

Chapter 6

1 What do the legal records on pages 32–39 tell us about people's religious beliefs in medieval times?
2 All sources used in this chapter come from court records. How would our understanding of crime be different if women criminals had left records?

Sources

General books used in all chapters

Gies, F. and J. *Women in the Middle Ages*, Barnes and Noble Books, 1980.

Kanner, B. (ed.) *The Women of England from Anglo–Saxon Times to the Present*, Mansell, 1980.

Power, E. (ed. Postan, M. M.) *Medieval Women*, Cambridge, 1975.

Stenton, D. *The English Woman in History*, Allen and Unwin, 1957.

Chapter 2

Register of Bishop Godfrey Giffard 1268–1301, quoted in Hair, P. (ed.), *Before the Bawdy Courts*, Elek Books, 1972.

A series of precedents and proceedings in criminal causes extending from the years 1475–1640, from the *Act books of the Ecclesiastical court in the Diocese of London*.

Chapter 3

Christine de Pisan, Quoted in Power, E. *Medieval Women*, Cambridge, 1975.

The Paston Letters (ed. Davis N.) Oxford, 1958.

The Household Book of Dame Alice de Bryene (ed. V. B. Redstone), quoted in *Dame Alice de Bryene*, W. and R. Chambers, 1977.

The Goodman of Paris (trans. Power, E.) Routeledge, 1928.

Letter from Dame Elizabeth Brew to Margaret Paston and letter from Joan of Pelham, from *A Medieval Post Bag*, (ed. Laetitia Lyell), Jonathan Cape, 1934.

The wills of Alice de Beaufow and Christina of Long Bennington, as quoted in *The English Woman in History* (op. cit.).

The wills of Lady Alice West and Lady Peryne Clanbowe, from *Earliest English Wills*, (ed. Furnivall, F.), Early English Text Society, 1882.

Chapter 4

The Will of Robert de Playce quoted in *Medieval English Nunneries* Power E., Cambridge, 1922.

Inventories of the Convents quoted in *Medieval English Nunneries* (op. cit.).

Visitation records quoted in *Medieval English Nunneries* (op. cit.)

Letter from Pope Eugenius to Hildegard of Bingen, quoted in *Women in the Middle Ages* (op. cit.).

Medieval Women (op. cit.)

Other books used in this chapter

Mulieres Sanctae, Brenda Bolton in *Women in Medieval Society* (ed. Susan Mosher Stuard) University of Pennsylvania Press, 1976.

Medieval Religious Houses: England and Wales Knowles and Hadcock, Longmans, Green and Co. 1953.

Chapter 5

The Vision of William concerning Piers the Ploughman, Langland, W. (ed. Skeat, W. W.), Oxford, 1886.

Nun's Priest's Tale, Geoffrey Chaucer (ed. Hussey, M.), Cambridge, 1965.

Christine de Pisan quoted in *Medieval Women* (op. cit.).

Indenture of Katherine Nougle to Avice Wodeford, 1392, Guildhall Library.

Calender of Plea and Memoranda Rolls of the City of London; Thomas, A. H. (ed.), London, 1929. (Volumes covering 1298–1468.)

Calender of Letter Books of the City of London, Vol. 1, Sharpe, R. R. (ed.), London, 1902.

'Hundred Rolls of 1274', as quoted in *Medieval Women* (op. cit.).

'The Lincoln Rule', as quoted in *Medieval Women* (op. cit).

Other books used in this chapter

Abram, A. *Women traders in Medieval London*, Economic Journal, No. 26, June 1916.

Bell, S. (ed.) *Women – from the Greeks to the French revolution*, Belmont, Caey, Wadsworth, 1973.

Hilton, R. (ed.) *Peasants Knights and Heretics: Studies in Medieval English Social History*, Cambridge, 1976.

Hilton, R. *English Peasantry of the Later Middle Ages*, Clarendon Press, 1975.

Chapter 6

Serjeanston, Rev. R. M. *Sanctuary Seekers in Northamptonshire*, Parts 1 and 2, in *Associated Architectural Societies Reports and Papers*, Vol. 32, 1913–14.

Hunnisett, R. F. *Bedfordshire Coroners Rolls,*
Bedfordshire Historical Society, vol 41, 1960.
Justices Itinerant Rolls 3, (PRO, JI3/125m 9d).
Justices Itinerant Rolls 3.
Given, J. B. *Society and Homicide in thirteenth century
England,* Stamford, California, 1977.
Justices Itinerant Rolls, 3, (JI3/48m 6).
King's Bench Rolls, (KB2, (PRO), KB 27/263M 32).
Northamptonshire Coroners' Rolls as quoted in
Serjeanston, Rev. R. M. (op. cit.)
Records of Manorial, Seigneurial and Church
Courts, as quoted in Hair, P. (ed.) *Before the
Bawdy Courts,* Elek Books, 1972.

Other books used in this chapter

Ehrenreich, B. and English, D. *Witches, Midwives
and Nurses,* Writers and Readers Publishing
Co-op, London, 1973.
Hanawalt, B. A. *Crime and Conflict in English
Communities: 1300–48* Harvard, 1979.
Kittel, R. *Women under the Law in Medieval England,
1066–1485* in Kanner, B. (ed.), (op. cit.).
Putnam, B. H. (ed.) *Proceedings before the J.P.s in the
Fourteenth and Fifteenth Century, Edward III–Richard
II.* Spottiswood and Ballentyne Co. Ltd, Ame
Foundation, 1938.

List of illustrations

The authors and publisher would like to thank the
following for permission to reproduce illustrations:

front cover, pp. 5, 7, 8 (above), 15, 17, 28 (above
right and below), 29 (above), 30, 33, 36, 37, 38
Bodleian Library; facing p. 1, pp. 25, 26, 27
Victoria and Albert Museum (prints supplied by
the photographic dept. Courtauld Institute of
Art); pp. 3, 8 (below), 9, 10, 11, 16, 19, 20, 22, 23
(below and right), 28 (above left), 29 (below), 32,
35 The British Library; p. 4 Bibliothèque
Municipale (print supplied by Giraudon); pp. 13,
14 Bibliothèque Nationale; p. 18 Alinari Museo
di Fotografie; p. 21 C.M.T. Assistance Publique;
p. 24 Musée Condé (print supplied by Giraudon).

Line drawing on p. 2 by John Blackman

Glossary

Alms	money given to charity, especially to help the poor	Meal	part of grain you can eat
Bailiff	lord of the manor's agent or foreman	Mercer	dealer in fabric and cloth
Baron	landowner who gets his land from the king in return for fighting for him	Novice	person learning to become a nun or priest
		Palfrey	saddle horse for ordinary riding, especially for ladies
Baxter	female baker	Peck	two gallons
Bind	tie up	Pewter	metal made of tin and lead
Holster	long, stuffed pillow	Porringer	small basin for soup, etc.
Boonwork	work peasants had to do on the lord's lands	Possett	drink of hot milk with ale, wine and spices
Bourderer	embroider	Presbytery	part of a church
Brewster	female brewer, maker of ale	Prophet	someone who reveals what God thinks
Buttery	place where food is kept	Provender	food, especially for horses and cattle
Card	prepare wool for spinning by combing it out	Quarter	28 pounds in weight
Cauldron	large saucepan for boiling	Regrate	to buy and re-sell something in or near original market, thus raising the price
Chattels	belongings		
Chronicle	record of event		
Comfit	sweet containing nut or seed in sugar	Repast	meal, feast
		Saffron	orange–yellow dye from crocus flower
Constable	early form of policeman		
Coverlet	bedspread	Sheaf	bundle of newly-reaped crop
Counterfeit	forge	Siege	surround a village, town, building forcing people inside to surrender
Disposition	arrangement		
Dowry	money or goods a woman's family gave to her husband on marriage	Shipwrights	shipbuilders
		Squire	someone who looks after and waits on a knight
Draper	seller of material		
Felon	criminal	Staff	long walking stick
Flesher	butcher	Surety	guarantee
Galingale	a root which tastes like ginger	Tallow	animal fat
Girdle	belt	Tenant	someone who rents a piece of land or property
Glean	harvest		
Hatchet	light, short-handled axe	Thatcher	someone who makes roofs out of straw or hay
Hospitaller	member of charitable, religious order		
		Thresh	beat corn to get out grain
Hovels	open shed, outhouse	Trivet	three-legged stand for holding a pot over a fire
Incontinency	having sexual intercourse		
Kempster	someone who combs out the wool	Violate	rape
		Vows	solemn promises
Leper	someone suffering from leprosy, a skin disease	Webster	female weaver
		Wimple	linen veil covering head and side of face and neck
Mace	spiked iron club		
Manor	lands owned by a lord	Winnowing	separate grain from husks by fanning
Mark(e)	coin worth 13s 4d		